Net bandits

by Ann Ruffell

Acknowledgements

Cover design: Oliver Heath, Rafters Design

Illustrations apart from pages 7 and 11 © **Paul Gardiner, 2005**. The right of Paul Gardiner to be identified as the illustrator of this work has been asserted by him in accordance with the Copyright, Design and Patents Act, 1988.

Brinsford books are a direct result of the findings of a two-year authoring/research project with young offenders at HMYOI Brinsford, near Wolverhampton. Grateful thanks go to all the young people who participated so enthusiastically in the project and to Judy Jackson and Brian Eccleshall of Dudley College of Technology.

First published in Great Britain by Axis Education Ltd

ISBN 1-84618-002-3

Axis Education PO Box 459
Shrewsbury SY4 4WZ

Email: enquiries@axiseducation.co.uk

www.axiseducation.co.uk

Jon was on the net.

He did it every day.

Log in. Chat a bit.

Log out.

Today the screen was red.

Then it was green.

Then it was little.

Then big.

Jon felt odd.

A man was in the screen.

He was not real.

But he looked real.

"Come in," said the man.

"You what?" said Jon. "Am I mad?"

"You are not mad," said the man. "Come on in."

"What is up?" said Ros.

"There is this man," said Jon.

"He is on the net."

He told his girlfriend Ros about it.

"You should have a good rest," said Ros.

She told Jon to come and sit down.

"But I could see him," said Jon.

"It is just a pop up," said Ros. "It will go away."

But it did not go away.

The next day the man was there again.

Just like before.

"Come in," said the man.
"It is a game. That is all.
Come on in."

This time Jon could not say no.
The screen went red.
Then it went green.
Jon put his hand on the screen.

It was like jelly.

His hand went past the screen.

He did not have to push.

"Where are you?" said Ros.

She saw his leg. That was all.

Then the leg was gone.

"Where am I?" said Jon.

There were lots more screens.

A ball went from one to the other.

Flip. Flip. All the time.

"What do you want with me?" said Jon.

There was no one to talk to.

There was only the ball.

He was stuck.

There was no way out.

Jon could not see the man.

He could only see the ball.

There was a pop,

then Jon was a bug.

He was in the ball.

He was in the ball with others.

They were all bugs.

"This cannot be," said Jon. "It is a dream."

But it was not a dream.

They had to go into the net.

The other bugs said what he had to do.

He could not say no.

He was a bug.

The others told him what to do.

He did as he was told.

It was only little to start with.

It was not hard.

Jon had to hack into programs.

He had to make them go bad.

It was just a bit of fun.

He could make a program crash.

He got good at it.

Jon could go into one of the screens.

He could swap bits about.

He could make the program go bad.

One day he began to see what he did.
He began to ask,
"What am I here for?"

Jon was not happy.
Some of his jobs might harm people.
"I cannot do this," he said.

23

His next job was on a big program.
Jon could see it would be bad.
He did not want to do it.
But he had to.

He saw the big firms go bust.
And when the big firms went bust,
the little firms went bust as well.

He saw Ros.

She had lost her job.

It was the bug that did it.

She was sad.

Jon was sad too, but he could not stop his jobs.

Next there was a plane crash.

They said it was a bug.

The bug was Jon.

But he could not stop. He had to go on.

There were clever men out there.

But they could not zap the bugs.

They could stop one bug.

But then the bugs were on to the next job.

Next there was a big job.

If they did it people would go to war.

Jon had to do it with the others.

"I do not want to do this," said Jon.

29

"You have to," said the other bugs.

"You have come so far, you cannot stop now.

We can make you go on."

One day he hit a tab and Ros was there.

"Ros! Help!"

"Come out, Jon," said Ros.

"I cannot," said Jon.

He did not want to tell her about the bad things he had done.

He told her about the ball.

He told her he was stuck.

"I will get you out," said Ros.

"Tell me the program."

But he could not tell Ros the program.

He had to get on with his job.

He put his task on the screen.

There was a way to stop the job.

He put it on the screen.

"Tell someone," he said.

But Ros did not want to do this.

She had to get Jon out.

She tapped at the keys.

The screen went red.

Then it went green.

Then it was little.

Then big.

The screen was like jelly.

Ros had to stop the bugs.

She had to get Jon out.

If she went into the screen they would get her
as well.
There was only one way.
"Switch off!" Jon yelled.

Ros pushed the button.
The screen went blank.

They were all safe.
But Jon had gone forever.

Glossary

ask	to say something as a question which you want answering
firms	companies that sell goods or services
girlfriend	a girl with whom you have a close, romantic friendship
green	the colour of grass
programs	set of instructions put in a computer
real	true, not false
war	when two or more countries fight each other